HOP O' MY THUMB

There once was a poor peasant and his wife who had seven sons. The youngest boy was very small for his age so they called him Hop o' my Thumb. However, Hop o' my Thumb made up for his small size by being very clever and when any of his family had a problem they would ask him for help.

But there was one problem that Hop o' my Thumb could not solve. His parents had very little money and it was often difficult for them to buy enough food to feed the boys.

One night, while his brothers were asleep, Hop o' my Thumb heard his mother sobbing in the next room. Hop o' my Thumb crept out of bed and went to listen at the door.

His father was saying: 'It's for the best, my dear. We haven't any money left and there is no more food in the house apart

from a piece of stale bread. The only thing we can do is to leave the boys in the middle of the forest tomorrow and hope that someone will take pity on them.'

Hop o' my Thumb thought about what he had heard. He found the piece of bread and went back to bed. Next day, the sad parents led the boys into the forest. Hop o' my Thumb walked a little distance behind the others, and dropped bread crumbs to leave a trail which the boys could follow to find their way back home.

After a long walk which led them into the thickest part of the forest, the peasant and his wife told the boys to pick some berries and look for firewood. Then the couple made their way back to their house, leaving the boys on their own.

At first the boys were happy to do as they had been told, but after a while they grew tired and wanted to go home.

'Follow me,' said Hop o' my Thumb, 'I know the way home.'

But when he looked for his trail of breadcrumbs, it had vanished. The birds had eaten every single crumb!

So Hop o' my Thumb told his brothers about their parents' plan to leave them in the forest. Some of the boys began to cry, but Hop o' my Thumb said, 'I know, I'll climb the highest tree I can find and try to see where we are.'

So the boys looked around and chose a high tree for Hop o' my Thumb to climb. When he had reached the highest branch he could get to, Hop o' my Thumb looked around. Not very far away he saw a large house and he hurried down the tree to tell his brothers about it.

The boys praised Hop o' my Thumb for being so clever and they made their way quickly to the house.

When the boys knocked on the door it was opened by a woman who looked very worried when she saw them.

'We're lost and we're hungry. Please would you give us a bite to eat and a bed for the night?' asked the eldest boy.

'Oh dear, oh dear,' said the woman, anxiously. 'My husband is an ogre and he will be home soon. If he sees you he will want to eat you for his breakfast.'

'Oh, please let us in,' begged the boys. They told her

about their poor parents and how they had left them in the forest because there was no food at home. If the boys stayed in the forest at night they were sure to be eaten by the wolves and bears.

At last the woman took pity on them and let them

into her house. She gave them a good meal and told them to get some sleep in the big spare bed.

After their long and frightening day, the boys soon fell asleep. They did not hear the ogre when he came home.

The ogre was in a bad mood. His wife cooked him a huge meal, but he grumbled that it was not enough.

'Bring me more meat, woman,' he shouted. 'And be quick about it!'

His wife hurried to fetch him some more food, frightened that he would wake the boys with his shouting.

When he had finished eating, the ogre sat picking his teeth. 'What is that smell?' he cried suddenly. 'I think I can smell human flesh. Who is in my house, wife?'

The ogre's wife did not dare to answer him. So the ogre got up and began to search the house. After looking in each room, he went into the room where the boys were sleeping. 'Ah ha!' he shouted. 'What have we here?'

The angry shouting woke the boys. Two of them leapt out of bed and tried to run between the ogre's legs. The ogre was too quick for them, however, and he caught one in each arm. 'Ho, ho, ho,' he roared. 'So this is where you are hiding. Well, I must say I would like some tasty young meat for my breakfast tomorrow. Unfortunately, I am too full to eat anything else just now.'

The ogre dropped the boys onto the floor and went out of the room. He locked the door and put the key in his pocket.

'What are we going to do?' sobbed one of the boys.

'Let's see if we can escape out of the windows,' said Hop o' my Thumb.

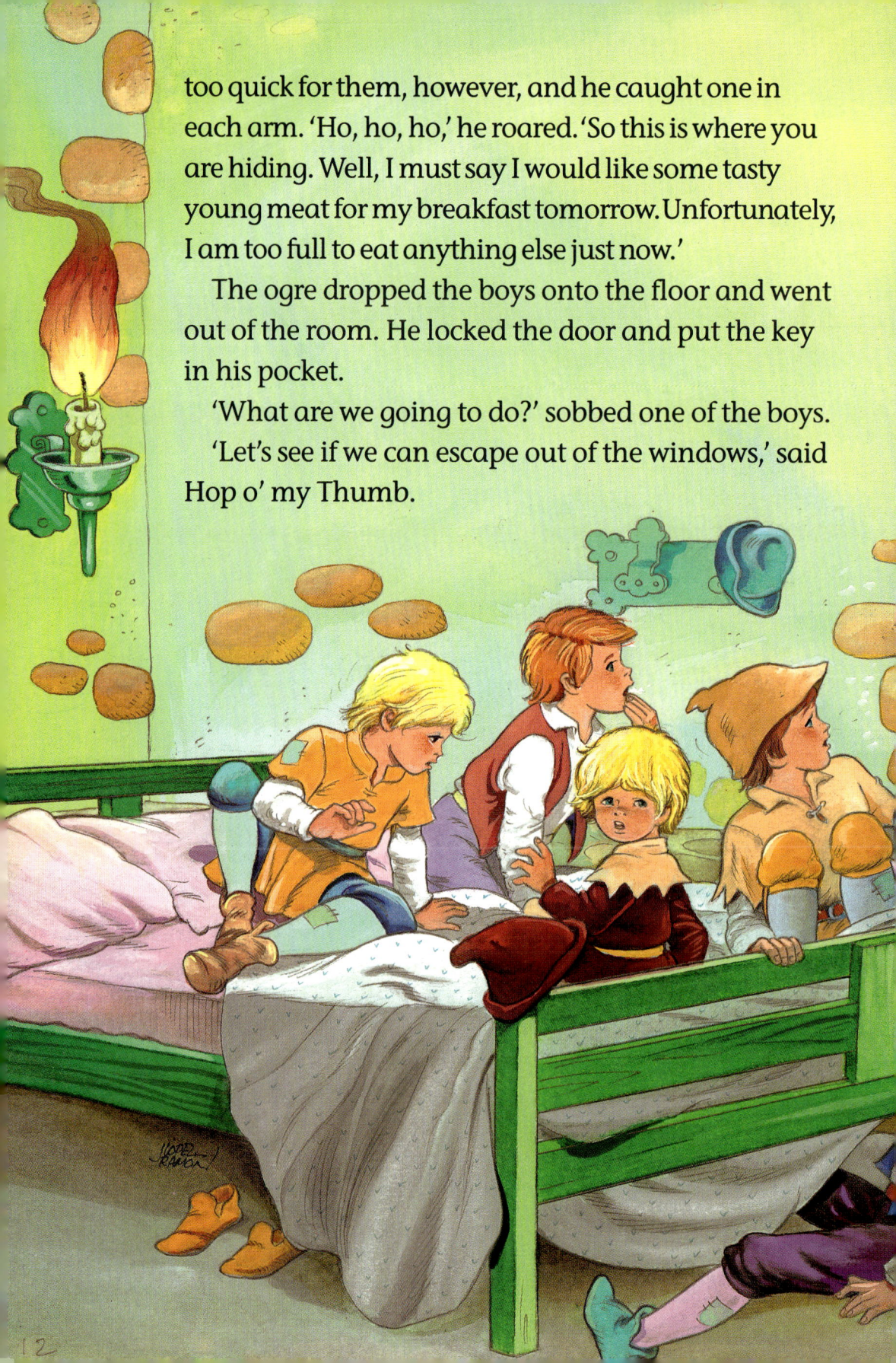

The boys opened a window and looked out. Unfortunately, however, their room was far above the ground and it was too high to jump from. When the brothers saw this they began to sob pitifully and to say their prayers. Only Hop o' my Thumb did not cry. He was busy trying to open the lock on the door with a pin. But the lock was too stiff and he could not manage it.

Instead, Hop o' my Thumb attempted to cheer up his brothers. 'Don't worry,' he said, 'we might be able to escape when the ogre comes into the room tomorrow morning.'

The next day, the ogre's wife got up early to light the fire in the oven. When she passed the door of the room where the boys were, she heard them sobbing and praying. The woman, who had no children of her own, took pity on the boys. She stole the key from the ogre's pocket and quietly unlocked the door. Then she let the boys out and whispered to them to go. 'Hurry away as fast as you can,' she said. 'When my husband wakes up and discovers that you have

escaped he will be furious. If he catches you, there won't be a second chance.'

'Thank you, kind lady,' said the boys, as they tiptoed out of the house.

Once in the forest the boys ran as fast as they could, tripping and stumbling in their haste to get

away. Sometimes, little Hop o' my Thumb had to be helped along because he was so small and could not run as fast as his brothers.

As soon as the ogre woke up he went straight to the room where the boys had been kept prisoner. He unlocked the door and saw that the room was empty. He looked in all the cupboards and under the bed, but he could not find the boys.

'Wife!' shouted the ogre. 'Where is my breakfast? Have you cooked the boys already?'

The woman was silent at first, for she was frightened of her husband's anger. But the ogre made her tell him what she had done.

'Well, those little boys won't escape me!' roared the ogre. 'I will wear my magic boots that cover seven miles in one stride. I'll soon overtake them and when I catch them I will make a nice big fire to roast them on.'

The ogre ran to the cupboard and pulled out his magic boots. When he had put them on he ran out of the house and into the forest. He could not see the boys, but he found their footprints on the ground.

'Ah ha!' he said to himself. 'So they ran this way. I will follow their trail and catch them up.'

The giant took a few strides in the direction of the boys' footprints, but he had forgotten that he was wearing his magic boots. In three strides he had overtaken the boys.

'Hmmm! Well I will just have to wait for them to pass this way,' thought the ogre. 'And when I see them coming I shall jump out and catch them.'

The ogre sat down. He felt sleepy in the warm sun and he

lay back, resting his head on a stone. He was soon fast asleep.

Not long after, the boys came running along the path that led past the sleeping ogre. When they saw him lying on the ground they thought he was dead. But as they came closer they heard a gentle snore and realised that the ogre was only sleeping.

'Ssssh, we must not wake the ogre,' warned Hop o' my Thumb.

The boys silently tiptoed over to where the ogre lay. Hop o' my Thumb whispered to them, 'Let's steal his boots so that when he wakes up he won't be able to follow us.'

The brothers all agreed that this was a good idea, so Hop o' my Thumb gently pulled the magic boots off the ogre's feet

and put them on his own. Of course, they were far too big for him, but Hop o' my Thumb stood up and took one stride. In an instant he had stepped seven miles and was out of sight. His brothers were very puzzled and did not know what had happened. In another moment, Hop o' my Thumb had reappeared! He told his brothers that the boots were magic.

'Guess what I have seen!' he said excitedly.

Hop o' my Thumb told his brothers that he had seen their mother and father's house, and that he knew the way there.

Before long, the boys were at home. The peasant and his wife were delighted to see their sons again. Although they were still poor, they had felt very sad without the boys.

Hop o' my Thumb showed his mother and father the magic boots. 'I will sell the boots for a lot of money,' he said.

Next day, he went to the nearest town and did just that. His family used the money to buy food and clothes, as well as enough animals to start a farm.